lemonworld & other poems

lemonworld
& other poems

carina finn

co•im•press
collaborative • cooperative • immediate
normal, illinois

published by co•im•press
normal, illinois
www.coimpress.com

manufactured in the united states of america

book design: alyssa bralower & co•im•press
cover design: co•im•press
production assistant: alyssa bralower
typeface: futura

isbn 978-0-9888199-1-7

CONTENTS

For my twinny <3.

PURR

oh my next fur will be nothing like my last fur.
to hell with "keep toasty and drink tea."
I want to go on a safari I might be afraid of.

SWEATMOTHER'S LADYKILLER MADE A HANDGRENADE IN WORKSHOP

fields of burlesque.
fields of joy & fields of burlesque.

don't trump the mode,
there's rabbit in the marshmallow !

nonaminals are buried in every open
lexicon.

THE GIRL IN A BLUE POLKADOT DRESS

fucking perfect. I got lost in the circus.
the bowtie can loveaway to oncemore days.

take a two-leaf flapjack in a giveaway jacket

& buy this rain to abort the red sahara !
with a soul herringbone & a pocketsnare face

all fashioncape memories
                    are rough around the beige.

TWINNING

a body is a car accident. like, a cardboard box is the bloodiest retraction. windowsided backbreaks are the preeminent tragedy. the age is lemonade. this is the horizon of modernity. a woodcut is plastified; the input is trimmed. masquerade! there is an age. like, who even uses sentences anymore.

VAN GOGH IS BIPOLAR

teenage riot, I thought the world of you.

collection B : the animals were gone.

collection B : pleats are nice

collection B : please smile.

forest green with a ray of sunshine,
you played my heart to the beat.

THISLOVE/THISHATE

french gamine brooklynite,
it's hip to be coral.

study the classics and get lost in the tutu.
let's not try to figure everything out all at once.

QUITE POSSIBLY ROCK & BORROW ROSE

firstgravesummer in the mood for leopard
& sepia virgins pink my dangerfresh forever.

american go†h left winterclothes in my skin

while some geek going greyscale pretended
genius meant too much.

good morning, school bitches,

f**k me. I am famouse !

STARSTRUKK

dress: basic space clinic wedges.
coat: southwestern fringe contrast.
tights: winter sunset lullaby.
boots: teenage crime.

ANYWHERE/WE GO

you're never alter, you're always nuclear.

because...

doc's befriending the junebug in the fireweed alley.

paperbag please so I say thank you for the boulevard.

new radicals, nautical nanobeings—

baby, that's my philosophy.

PUNCTUATE PLEASE !

this browniemix in me makes me wanna die.

COLORBOMB!

lazy linepainter dressed herself in june.

birthdayinthewoods,

got those rainy blackandgreys...

architectural dresses divide

the deadmetal circus.

disarming dollie! not another comadarling.

PRETTY HANDSOME AWKWARD

swallowed in the "hello autumn!"
historybooks shake through my pretend friends.

bittersweet turquoise changes everything—
and I don't believe in buttercup gold

OPIUMFAVOUR

faceless djette maquillage pas?
vive la fête ! it's a mightyfine movie.

rosetrouble busted a sunfight flyby

fevered to blue
like a lazerweeked crystalized ▲

CREATURE FROM THE SKY WITH DIAMONDS

cherries, ribbons, and rainbows go all to bits b/c
the devil makes us sin where the wild girls live.

velvet-turbaned socialite stuffed with triangle
cobra kryptonite, you're flagged for deletion on the
cemetery drive &

everyone's hoping for hell except me.

LITTLEFLOWERS

I wish I could feel infinite
preobjectmorning.

these ghostkids are such a disgrace.
I need an older crowd.

KNEELOVIN' CITY OF DARKNESS

sexforbreakfast in the special village.
I wear shirtpants when I apply

sixfeetundersigh & starryeyed...

we cave new lines one cup at a time.

o, heartsrevolution!
                                        a darkishday.

DAAAD, I TOOK YOUR SHIRT, OK !

the color of our grunge vibes is who cried wolf.
let's chop some wood in the rubymountains.
ooo ooo ooo, I just wanna groove—
dead animal & run the black buckle blooming!

LACE + SKATES

speak to the wind like an anchor on my heart.
kiss & resolve to wink, by golly.

hey little swimming pond,
peace is a field of graves.

french navy, I have to kill you. I want hot, sunny, etc.

LEMONWORLD

ambulances arabesque on the fire escape and quote the collaboration flask. discrepancy is a complicated windowshade. alternately, the bridge is a real imaginary. walloping whatever. dumbest mountainside is the fondest allegory. juandiced afternoon, alabaster is a stupid queue. love is assisted rughelach. nox lox. a bit of tidewater.

hominy o hominy my heartbox ate a harpie. to hollaback an ectoplast it has to have a larkbreak.

my hatred of the wunderland is snow snow snow. a streetcar named a liar is a lifelong show. back in the barstool the kitchenette was concrete. a teapot mouse equated aligned. I was quite satisfied. when she was seventeen, brooklyn was a prairie.

CAIRO, Y R U SO CRUELLL xXxX

emptysleep, where did you go?
last night's party was fueled by balloons.

saturday killed the featherdance star
w/ maxikultur breaklights

so we cutwrist & purr.

boyish girlinesses bury woodhouse tools
bc such tan moods only love newrules.

METALCORPSE

demi-curve, demi-skinny, demi-love a latte.
wonderstruck in platinum; a basket case
right on the dot. sheer vs. leather vs. soft vs.
hard. drink the doors now—if I am then just
say. slashed on the dancefloor reminds me
to pray. never without my autumn sunshine!
we must make a peace sign to the world.

THE ELSEWHERE WISH

demicat, let's sail away to slouchy;
slowly recall your cozyhood bangs.

no function please,
northern flashdam in the sky.

all a crustacean needs is snow.

IMAGINATION IS THE REFORMATION MEDICINE

toggle coke & whisky
ready 2 start new layers
saturdaydeep in 2mrw's
yesterday.

silk shearling plays
the new wannabe
for 99 cents & a catscarf
in advance.

oldphonewonder,
do you have the time?
ultraviolet moths
only flower at midnight.

rabbit-hearted girl,
you must be a symbol of
the revolution.

PHOTOWALK IN RAINCOUVER

cold cold cold is around the monochromatic!
I'm living in the alarm of a handgrenade swing.

dear holiday sequins, girly mature is a faux skin.

no such thing as fake, this trick we have of
turning vixen.

BEDHAIR

it was windy
and I was like
baby
baby
baby...
ooooh.

techno angst is a rocket to the moon.
sway, misfortunes. jamais vu. I got you.

FANCYTREEHOUSE

I found all kinds of historical documents,
sunshine and lollipops, coffee and novels.

a 22-year-old slumberdoll gave me fleas.

cosmic poppies golden for fall flashback
the sp-sp-sparkly sun.

GREY DAY OH YES

if you leave me I'll still have
my indulgent routine:
abbreviated winds litter
fall fall fall.
mrs.wooly was not comfortable
and very hot.
is it sunny where you are?
forest boys turn my swag on.

WORK

young lady in jeans, hide your face!
be the change you wish to see.

16-year-old girl looking to buy a moustache,
the horses are free animals.

AFTER VERY PARTY I DIE.

current obsession—waisting my time
current mood—beamin'
wearing—flies
listening to—a velvet heat wave

good news, flotsam!
the blues full of grace blog you.

MODERN PRINCESS

awkward violet business-class dancing melts
your rock-heart castle like a cheerful chickadee.
androgynous shooting star, here we are!
it was fear of myself that made me odd.

PLEATED HEROIN

thou high ghostly
incarnation fleshly living,
I conceived a mighty
hazelnut—

quick & lively

& hideous.

POPPY POPPY POPPY #3

I fell down the garage sale, baby blue.
denim stripes + brown + old white art
= hearts. sunshine lady, love is grand.
divorce is a pair of headphones.

the velvet definition is insanity.
the video's title is miracle of life.

AFTERNOON ZEST
IN A HAPHAZARD EVERYWHERE

something different—a spring feeling !

grooveking, anyone can tap my heart.

doublemercy pushing kiddo,
photograph me to nowhere

& triarevolution in a sea of pastel cups.

PRETTYBOY SWAG

pixie queen of the bible club,
this world is not good for me.

decadent ballerina,
I'm fine without you.

there's a tennis dress
and she's down by the river—

cherrysnack,
don't hurt my stroll by the bridge.

I'M NOT AN ABACUS BUT YOU CAN COUNT ON ME

my birthday diet: chocolates & cigarettes at se-ven-A.M.

out of focus bunny, smell the project in the air—
billionaire smokin' mirrors in a batzone wonderlair.

let's get lost mcqueen, I'm the new bob dylan
but you're still the one when the weather is porcelain.

SNAP/GLAMOROUS

forgot my green grass in the city...
a stranger's heart will blow dirty rich.

why discipline peaches & cream
when we may stumble upon a carousel?

STILL WORK SO HARD

build politics in space brick by boring brick
to salute the dying race who makes it always.
townlife lovey-love like a dead camel coat
& try to take my bag underneath the mistletoe.

BLOODY WINTERTIGER I'M A ROCKETEER!

internal sunset dreamsicle,
we'll fill our mouths with cinnamon now.

OLD-FASHION MORPHINE

call me that grey door.
rainbow mickystems style mayhem in pettidots.

ladyboss debating plaid sunwings,
dream a little truth with grace;

simple lifestyle out to lipstick with my fans &
feed the copper wire to the present-tense lullaby.

COLOURS LIKE WEAPONS IN TRAGICBLOODY BEETROOTS

roses are red,
there's no such thing as the world.

this is my version of a holy shirt.

AUTOBIOGRAPHICIDE

the piñata polka dots the foundry like gold dust,
red and red and denim again.

little blue riding hood dreams the winter scarf.
no sleep till rainy days wildfox the blackberries.

$HIT HAPPENS PINK PANTHER

in through your escape will fall the sky.
animal arithmetic is chic 4life.

cast me quietly unto morning's light.
how many castles whisper goldblood in the wild?

QUIT MICROWAVING YR EYES OUT

happy bird-day ribwillow girl !
cream + nude is a supercomfy food.

goodwasted to coatwalk you sexy
little swine.

nastyblue thou art,

                    & intensely coming—

LONG LIVE MCQUEEN

excuse my black veil, I am off to paint.

ARE YOU TRYING TO LOOK UNNATRACTIVE, ZOOBOY?

fashion enjoys the perverse
& lazy doubleviolent closet raid.

WITHOUT A SHRED OF EVIDENCE

little green riding hood is an addict
from the past.

the life of a professional butterfly catcher
is constantly changing shape.

COSMIC POPPIES

caterpillar girl, believe in the things you know:

teapots, ruffles,
vintage prussian;
frozen sunshine
and cherry tears.

the limeshorts paint it blood and chocolate.
would you really rush out on me now?

TEQKILLA

eminence front miss nothing!
insert wise statement here.
cigarettes, weddingbands, weblogs, etc.
terminally chill heroin-chic smoker,
company's coming.

PEACHYTIME TRAVELS THE ORPHANED LOVECHILD

you bet your someday valentine.

go ahead and jump !

don't abort yourself in thisdress.

GIRL IN TIE

festival fashion for the lads is bow and snow
but pocahontas likes the duffel coat.

if it means a lot to you it makes me wanna die.
I'd rather fuck. I hate the cold.

A VERY LAZY BAGELDAY

cameraflash asap plzzz !! & take a lace straight
through my brain.

because the sky is mink it's a taffy sunset.

if you're a bird, I'm a bird!

u + me together = stars 4ever.

THIS BLANKET OF SNOW KEEPS ME WARM

little bird, a lady does not own outrage!
you had a flame for your white pony, for your
black caviar...

backyard gladiator, I do not have joyous eyes.
all around me lighted deer nutcracker *en nude*.

a la mode is little minx voodoo.
stranger, I'm so obsessed with sable.

boy london is a toxin. I'm so obsessed with greys.

ROSES ARE DAYDREAM, SORBETS ARE PINK

not to touch the bird so u put an earth on it.

goldenpony, dust the phoneme.

CRUEL SLACK TIDE, PUT YOUR RECORDS ON

hello hurricane, you are not enough.
safety pins are holding up the world beneath you.

bare failure teaches a wrecked man computer love.
ace questioningly. I'll fly with you, café americano.

LEMONWORLD II

sunny winter—hide your eyes!
monday ashes chernobyl child.

lost : jupiter marilyn knit cardigan
leaving flying propane nightmares.

kaboom!
let me play the violin for you.

+*+*IWANNAROCKBLACK

yes, 1986—blossomback my student things;

different sensations let it roll in darkshadow.

glowcream fuck in the morning, natural,

& bad pizzaid from the frozen bandwagon.

A RIVER FLOWS IN YOUR </3
IT'S A CRUEL, CRUEL WORLD

sunny days, I'm coming from your tears.
the first sip of fringe is always the best.

there's a limit to your love
& I want you to quit.

it's not a war, it's a renegade silence.

XXXO

moonset on wood like punching in a dream.

MY SERIOUS VIRGIN MARY TAPESTRY

whisper something sweet, ginger snow cake.
in lack of control, spread the light like home.
doubt shades of cosby to chasm your sympathy.
my name is christmas, will you merry me?

CUPCAKEKISS

secret blumercury vampire from london,
double denim + pink nails = untamed fireflies.

windblown leather steals the synthetic prince.
swallow on the trees, I hope this takes you too.

TOO LATE FOR LITTLECLOUD

lazy shakeit killed my baby
whimsical-pale, another day at dawn.
girlworld can burn a towntrip quick.
o,
                    let's just paris away.

+*+*CLARITY

raise your stars & teacups
for the girl w/ red specs.

MINTY ADVENTUREFAIR

gold sequins in the dark places. just an ordinary day
& I don't know what to do with myself.

after we lost la vie en rose the nudevelvets valentined
like 1, 2, 3.

o, princess of darkness of this world !

do you want the real thing

or are you just talking??

THIS SUMMER I WORE THIS

dog days can't say no to leopard
so the diamond lentils bloom another winter.

mixing prints is lost in translation.
forest winds shouldn't sparkle but they do.

VINTAGEVIRGIN

when you wake you'll have cake
8-year-old fashion junkie.

basic wandering varsities change shape
& cry, baby—

you're in one. when the sun goes down
we'll charcoal again.

lovely day, bunny,
but who will stop this tiresome rain?

DIRTYHAIRHALO

you've got the instinct wild honeypie.
standing in the humbug I'm a map of your head.
vodka-cran found you in a vintage sock.
I love this place but it's haunted by da vinci.

JEANS JEANS JEANS

snack on stripes and mirrors
with all the pretty little horses.

divine project, running away.

it's all burgundy

        but it's not easy to know.

HEARTFIXER

the 11th dimension is very summery.

tiny phantom from my nightmares,
I've got a bike. you can ride it if you'd like.

LABYRINTHEAR

life's good nightlight.
runaway, close your eyes;

bagraiders bring you
fearflowers,

cometbooks,

pink winter secondhands
of the ones we love.

FUTUREDUST

it's too warm for this mermaid skull.
I would make an excellent pirate.

wild west rainpunch ends in a frame—
can't trust an audience of one these days.

MY MOJO SO DOPE

nudecoffeebreakdown knee high in changing channels.

stockholm syndrome thrifted, gifted.
pushingnotice,   I don't feel it.

LEOCAPE

you've got too much to wear on your story,
darling—

you know wildcat marks won't break my heart.

goodbye twist fringe & crochet iceage!
inside of a raindrop the sun is beautiful.

GET UP AND GO!

forgot my pants in the city.
blockdot yellow details on the rise.

hold on tight to undecided.
go east, good twin. got a lust for life.

VELVETDAY

best wishes, black swan.
I can't forget the swim to reach the end.
holy exile sings like ooh.
my rouge dress is a postcard from far away.

FEATHERSKIRT & HEARTFUR

little bridges pretty in fog like the ruin of st. paul
stuck with lilac thorns.

the neutral queen is so naïve &&

the black sheep is a gumsicle that won't come home.

sweetasglass, bone the floralsunshineplayland.
channeling my face is gonna break your miracles.

ACKNOWLEDGMENTS

Thanks C. J. Waterman and Johannes Göransson for being smart, generous, and supportive readers/editors, the people of Cairo for being bratty in the best possible way, and Kayla Finn for being my twin and letting me write this entire book on your bed. Special thanks for the generous support received from The Winter Break Residency of My Mom's House.